QUILT DESIGNS

FROM

NATIVE AMERICAN POTTERY

DR. JOYCE MORI

American Quilter's Society
P.O. Box 3290 • Paducah, KY 42002-3290
Fax 270-898-1173 • e-mail: orders@AQSquilt.com

MW00998507

Located in Paducah, Kentucky, the American Quilter's Society (AQS) is dedicated to promoting the accomplishments of today's quilters. Through its publications and events, AQS strives to honor today's quiltmakers and their work and to inspire future creativity and innovation in quiltmaking.

Executive Book Editor: Andi Milam Reynolds
Graphic Design: Lynda Smith
Cover Design: Michael Buckingham
Quilt Photography: Charles R. Lynch

Additional copies of this book may be ordered from the American Quilter's Society, PO Box 3290, Paducah, KY 42002-3290, or online at www.AmericanQuilter.com.

Text © 2013, Author, Dr. Joyce Mori
Artwork © 2013, American Quilter's Society

Library of Congress Cataloging-in-Publication Data

Mori, Joyce.
  Quilting Designs from Native American Pottery / By Dr. Joyce Mori.
       pages cm
  Includes bibliographical references and index.
  Summary: "Traditional, contemporary and art quilters will find these historic and prehistoric designs inspired by Native American pottery widely adaptable. Use these more than 100 designs in many ways: Embroidery designs, painted fabric motifs, paint stick patterns, appliqué designs, threadwork, and beading patterns"--Provided by publisher.
  ISBN 978-1-60460-059-9 (alk. paper)
  1. Quilting--Patterns. 2. Textile design--Themes, motives. 3. Indian decoration and ornament--Themes, motives. I. Title.
  TT835.M685 2013
  746.46--dc23
                    2013004514

ACKNOWLEDGMENTS

I have been so fortunate to be able to pursue my love of quilting for over 20 years. I wish to thank the American Quilter's Society for publishing many of my books. The publication of my first book, *Quilting Designs from Native American Designs*, launched my quilting career. I have worked with AQS editors and graphic artists through the years and it has always been a pleasure. I thank the current executive book editor, Andi Reynolds, for her interest in my designs, which has resulted in this new book.

I have enjoyed all my visits to quilt conferences and guilds throughout the years. I have met many wonderful quilters who have enjoyed my work and encouraged my creative pursuits.

I owe my interest in quilting to my mother. I only wish she could have been alive to see the quilts I have created. Both my parents always supported my academic achievements and encouraged my hobbies. My father was alive to see many of my publications and quilts, and for that I was blessed.

My wonderful husband, John, has always been encouraging and helpful. We went through college and graduate school together and worked on research projects side by side. He has often offered helpful advice on my quilt projects and has taken countless photographs for me through the years.

My daughter, Susan, who is highly skilled with computers, took up quilting a number of years ago and she helped me understand what she wants in machine-quilted designs. My love has always been hand quilting, so her input was most valuable. We share an interest in several crafts and that has brought about some fun trips and adventures.

I also thank all the magazine editors and publishers who have been supportive through the years. Every article or book is a learning experience, and as long as I can learn, I feel I can enjoy life to the fullest.

And finally, I owe a debt of gratitude to all the Native American craft persons, most of theme anonymous, who have produced such wonderful pieces of art from prehistoric times to the present. Their mastery of techniques and their use of design and color have meant they have given us a collection of wonderful objects to study and appreciate. I am in awe of their work whenever I see it.

CONTENTS

INTRODUCTION

DESIGN HINTS

MACHINE QUILTING SYMBOLS

RECOMMENDED BOOKS

GALLERY

HAND QUILTING DESIGNS

MACHINE QUILTING DESIGNS

ABOUT THE AUTHOR

Original art tile, 6"x 6", by Gale Tu-oti, Tucson, Arizona, 1996

INTRODUCTION

I have been using Native American motifs in quilting designs for many years. This new book provides readers with more examples of these wonderful designs.

These designs are intended for use in more than Native American-themed quilts. Most of them are suitable for all types of quilts, from contemporary to traditional.

Although I really enjoy hand quilting, there are a number of designs for machine quilters. The machine quilting designs accommodate continuous line and free-motion quilting. Please remember that most of the machine quilting designs can be hand quilted.

Where known, I have included the tribal affiliation for the designs. If the tribe is not known, I have included the region, known as a culture area, of the design source. Basically, a culture area is a geographical area with somewhat uniform environmental conditions. The tribes that resided within them adapted in similar ways to that environment.

Anthropologists differ somewhat on the exact boundaries of culture areas and the specific tribes within them, but for my purpose, they are used to provide the reader with a general location for the designs' origin or place of use. If you want to know more about culture areas and the tribes in each, just use a search engine and type in "Native American Indian culture areas."

I have provided dates for designs when I could, but such information is often not available. Dating often becomes a subjective estimate by scholars.

I do not copy an entire design from the original source and use it in my quilting designs. Rather, I select an individual motif from a given Native American object and I rework the motif into a completely new design.

I do not select any of my designs from current craftworks in order not to infringe upon any copyrights. However, if you study Native American craftwork, you will soon notice that current craftpersons often utilize motifs from historic

and prehistoric items. We both recognize that older design motifs can be used in modern projects.

I have provided both straight line and curvilinear designs. As you study the pictures in the Gallery, you will see there are uses for the designs in addition to their primary use as quilting motifs. I feel very strongly that Native American cultural items are a wonderful source of inspiration for quilters, and I hope you will enjoy using the designs on your quilts.

I believe my use of Native American-derived motifs serves to promote a respect for and appreciation of the cultures and arts and crafts of all native peoples. Native American tribes and ethnic people around the world are struggling to maintain their identities; it is important for all of us to recognize the richness and value of other cultures (life ways) and people and their contribution to our existence.

DESIGN HINTS

I have a few general comments concerning the designs:

- You will probably need to enlarge or reduce the designs to fit the specific space on your project. Sometimes when a design is enlarged there is more blank space than you might want. Just add crosshatching or other fill as desired. Likewise, if you reduce a design, you might need to remove some of the design's lines so the quilting lines are not too close together.

- On some of the designs for machine quilters I have added dashed lines to indicate possible areas for fill. Sometimes I added a central spiral motif to a machine quilting design. This could obviously be removed if desired. But likewise, a center fill could be added to any motif with an empty center space. All these decisions become your own personal design choices.

- Many of the designs can be used for projects other than quilting. They can be used as embroidery designs, fabric painted motifs, paint stick patterns, appliqué designs, and thread stitching patterns. They might also be embellished with beadwork. The samples shown in the Gallery offer you inspiration for your own projects.

- Some designs are not drawn as bilaterally symmetrical though they appear as if they should be. The native craft workers drew the designs freehand, so both sides were not always exactly symmetrical. Some of my designs reflect this; I feel it adds more interest and uniqueness to the designs.

MACHINE QUILTING SYMBOLS

Start ●   Direction ❯   Stop |

On the designs created for machine quilters, a starting point is marked. This start point is flexible in many cases. You may prefer to start at the left or right side of the design or the top or the bottom. The direction arrows show you how the design progresses; you should alter it to fit your own style of movement.

RECOMMENDED BOOKS

I have not included directions on the technical aspects of how to machine or hand quilt. There are many excellent books available that discuss these techniques in detail. Readers would be best served to read one or more of them if you have never machine or hand quilted, or if you wish to improve your techniques:

That Perfect Stitch: The Secrets of Fine Hand Stitching
by Dierdra A. McElroy (Breckling Press, 2011)

Guide to Machine Quilting
by Diane Gaudynski (AQS, 2002)

Machine Quilting: A Primer of Techniques
by Sue Nickels (AQS, 2003)

GALLERY

I have created several items that show this book's designs used for items other than quilts.
I hope these examples will lead you to find other creative uses for these quilting designs.

PAINTED FRONT TOTE BAG

The front of this bag is a piece of tea-dyed muslin. It can be difficult to see the designs through the tea-dyed fabric so you might find it easier to use a piece of plain muslin for your first bag.

Select several individual designs and draw them on a piece of tissue paper that is the size you want for the tote bag front. Add fill units of circles, swirls, triangles, zigzags, etc., around and between the separate motifs. Use a light box to transfer the designs to the muslin using a permanent black marker.

I drew only the main motifs on the background. The fill motifs were painted freehand in areas between the major motifs. Paint the main motifs in colors of your choice. Let paint dry. Embroider around all the main motifs with a running stitch using 2 strands of embroidery floss. Seal the bag front by brushing a coat of Golden® Gel Medium over the front of the bag.

Sew your tote bag as you would normally. The example bag is lined. The beaded button accent is the center of a bead embroidery pendant, which is sewn at the base of one strap.

FABRIC CUFF

I love bracelets! This fabric cuff bracelet features thread stitching, hand embroidery, and beadwork. Instead of thread stitching the motifs, you could hand embroider or appliqué them. My bracelet has a medium thick stabilizer between the front and back to provide some stability to the piece. The bracelet is 2" wide x 8¾" long.

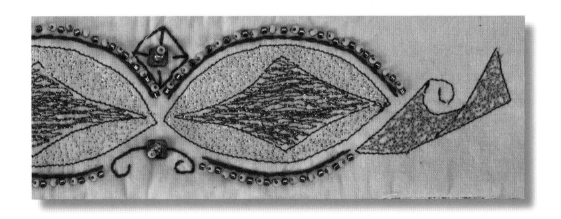

BALL CAP WITH MACHINE APPLIQUÉ

Select several motifs and machine appliqué them to a ball cap. The machine appliqué is somewhat challenging to complete when you use a purchased cap as I did. If you hand appliquéd the motifs, it would be easier. Likewise, placing the motifs a little further away from the brim would make the job easier.

T-SHIRT WITH HAND-EMBROIDERED MOTIFS

Fabric strips featuring Native American designs were sewn to the front of the t-shirt. Single Native American motifs were hand embroidered in a running stitch below the strips. Isolated Native American designs were cut out and machine appliquéd on the back of the t-shirt.

TOTE BAG
USING PAINT STICKS

I made a stencil of one of the motifs (page 47) and followed the directions for using Shiva® Artist's Paintstiks® to paint the motif on a background fabric. I added a gold paint, star-like design in the center. This tote bag also features a beaded button and free-form crochet motifs on the flap and on the bottom front. I used clear monofilament thread to meander quilt around the painted motif.

HAND-EMBROIDERED POTTERY VESSEL MOTIF TOTE BAG

The hand embroidery was completed with 2 strands of embroidery floss. I did machine stitching around the outside of the vessel motif and around several of the interior design motifs to secure the front to the thin batting between the front and the lining. Ribbon trim was sewn in place at each corner. The top border on the bag features machine appliqué around several Native American motifs. Some of the motifs were cut from fabric; others were printed photo transfers. Stamped designs and words complete the top band.

THREAD-STITCHED TOTE BAG

Thread stitching and basic machine stitching were used to outline and fill in one of the designs in the book (page 29). The design was slightly adapted for the tote bag. Fabric fringe cut on the bias and raw-edge fabric squares with buttons in the center were added to decorate the bag front.

MACHINE APPLIQUÉ SMALL WALL QUILT

The center block of this quilt is paper fabric. This is a piece of muslin that has been painted with a 1-to-1 ratio of water and white glue. Pieces of tissue paper were placed on the glue surface and more glue was painted over the tissue paper to be sure it was secured to the muslin. The tissue paper wrinkles as it is laid down and you achieve ridges and lines on the surface.

Pearlescent powders were sprinkled on the tissue paper surface while it was still wet. Once this dried, it was cut to shape and motifs were machine applied in place. Additional lines were drawn between the motifs with a permanent marker. The main center motif is on page 33.

After the borders had been sewn to the center block, additional motifs were appliquéd in place randomly. This block would also make a unique tote bag front.

SWEATSHIRT WITH MACHINE APPLIQUÉ MOTIFS

The sweatshirt was cut down the center front. The bottom ribbing was removed so the jacket would hang straight. Fabric borders were sewn on the center fronts and along the bottom. This added stability to the edges. Various Native American motifs were machine appliquéd along the front of the jacket.

PAMPHLETS

Watercolor paper was used for the cover; washes of beige, white, gray, and brown craft paints create the background. Wire embellishments, beads, designs drawn with markers, stamping, and painted motifs create the background interest.

The inside of the cover was a page of text from an old book. A wash of paint over-stamped with a commercial stamp and wirework grid was added.

T-SHIRT WITH FRAYED-EDGE BLOCKS

A basic pottery vessel shape with a single motif placed on the vessel was hand embroidered on each rectangle of tea-dyed muslin. A narrow fabric border was sewn to each block. Each unit was machine stitched to the t-shirt.

I stitched multiple times around the outside edge of each rectangle. I machine stitched around each vessel so the patch would not pucker. After machine washing, each patch developed frayed edges.

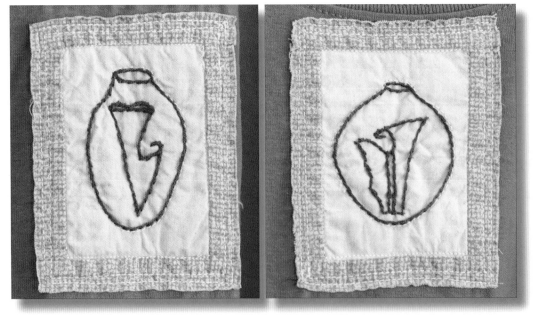

CHRISTMAS TREE SKIRT

The four corner panels are hand-embroidered motifs. The panels were combined with a batik fabric in Southwestern colors and with Southwestern motifs. The colors of the embroidery threads match colors in the fabric. The panels could also be embroidered in reds and green. Even though a design is Native American in origin, it does not have to appear Native American in the final project.

CHRISTMAS WREATH ORNAMENTS

Several motifs were copied onto a beige fabric using a light box. They were hand embroidered. Beaded accents were added to some. The other oraments were made by cutting motifs from commerical fabrics with Native American motifs.

WOOL FELT APPLIQUÉ
POTTERY VESSEL

Elements from several vessels were adapted to create this appliqué. Pottery vases in this style were originally made in the 1930s for the tourist market. I spent time on the Hopi reservation doing graduate reasearch and this piece is a personal reminder of that time. This could be framed or used as the front panel of a tote bag.

CANDLE MAT

The background circle was cut from an old wool shirt belong to my dad. Wool felt appliqués were machine sewn in place. I used only floral motifs.

HAND QUILTING DESIGNS

**Cree Beadwork
late 1800s**

Ojibwa Beadwork

Acoma Pottery

**Santo Domingo
Pottery
late 19th to early
20th century**

**Wasco
Beadwork
early 1900s**

Ojibwa Beadwork

**Montagnais
Birchbark**

**Cree
Beadwork**

Zuni Pottery and San Ildefonso Pottery

Zia Pottery

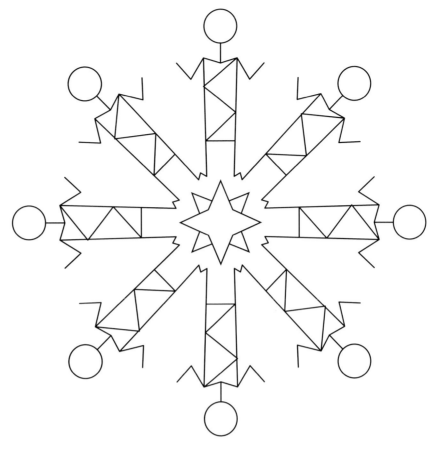

**Plains Indian
Rock Art**

Ojibwa Beadwork

Southwest Pottery

Navajo Rug

Hopi Pottery and Prehistoric Southwest Pottery

Acoma Pottery

Zuni Pottery

**Northeast
Woodlands
Beadwork**

**Socorro Olla
950AD–1400AD**

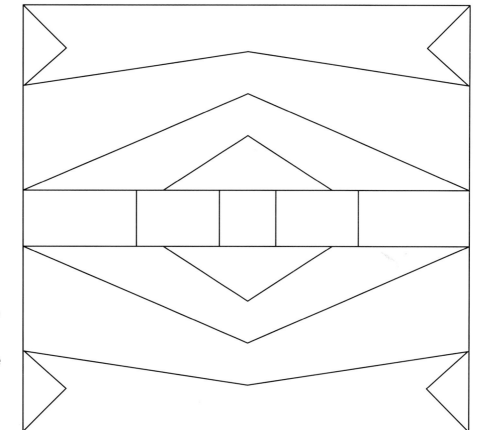

**Plateau
Parfleche
late 1800s**

A parfleche is a
carrying case or
storage container made
from a piece
of rawhide.
Geometric designs were
painted on them.

**Wyandot Beadwork
1825–1850**

**Creek or Seminole
Beadwork
early 19th century**

Southwest Pottery

**Hopi Pottery and
Zuni Pottery**

**Potawatomi and
Iroquois Beadwork**

Zia Pottery

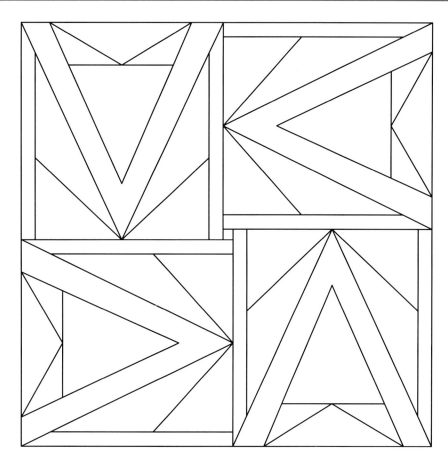

**Plains Indian
Parfleche**

**Southwest
Prehistoric Pottery**

**Kiowa Beadwork and
Cree Beadwork
on Moccasins
early 1900s**

**Haida Carving
late 19th century**

**Northeast
Woodlands
Beadwork**

**Hopi Pottery
early 20th century**

Hopi Pottery

**Santo Domingo
Pottery
late 19th century**

**Spokane Beadwork
early 1900s**

Hopi Kachina-style Motif
This is not an actual Kachina. I combined
elements from several styles of Kachina to
create this representation.

J.M.

Southwest Pottery

**Metis Beadwork and
Acoma Pottery**

**Triangle Unit
Iroquois
Beadwork**

**Paiute Basket and
Navajo Rug
early 20th century**

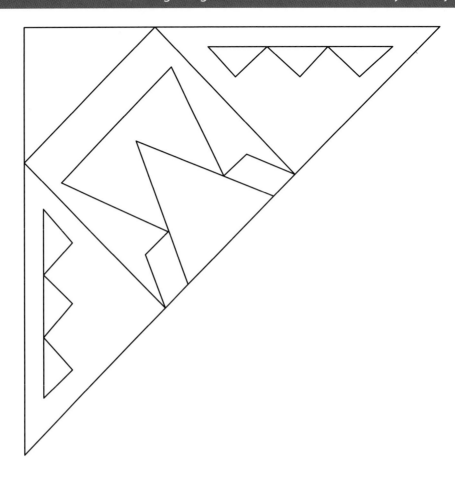

**Paiute Basket and
Navajo Rug
early 20th century**

Hopi Kachina-style Motif
This is not an actual Kachina. I combined
elements from several styles of Kachina to
create this representation.
J.M.

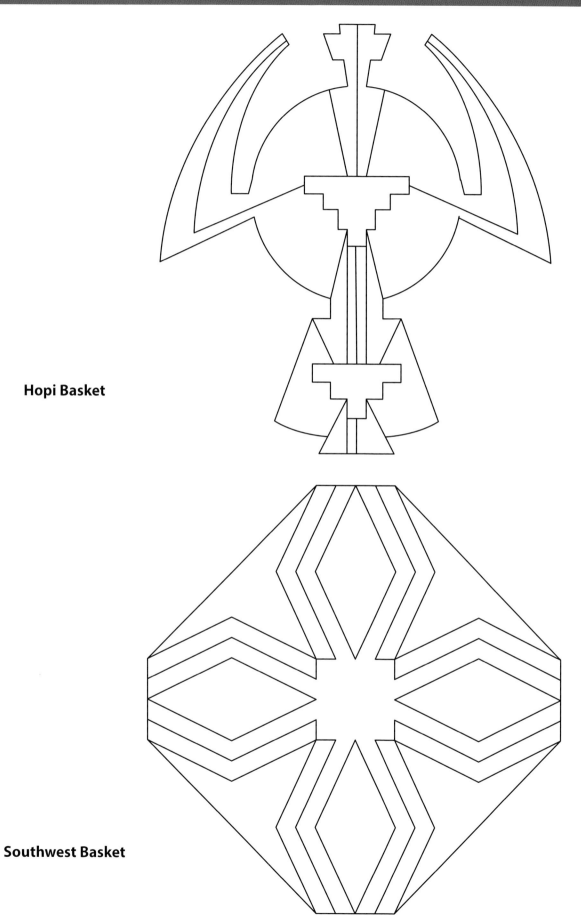

Hopi Basket

Southwest Basket

**Crow Beadwork
late 19th century**

**Montagnais
Birchbark**

San Ildefonso Pottery

Seminole Beadwork c. 1825

Ojibwa Beadwork

**Santo Domingo
Pottery
1930s**

Hopi Pottery

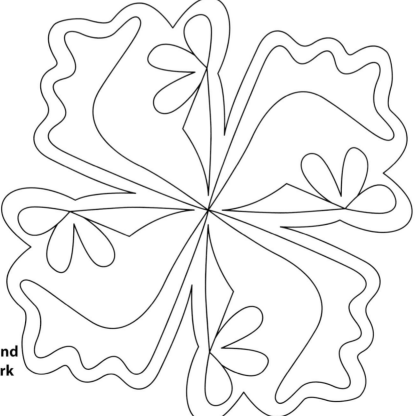

**Zuni Pottery
late 19th century and
Delaware Beadwork
late 1800s**

An example of a Southwest Pottery vessel created for quilters

Southwest Pottery

MACHINE QUILTING DESIGNS

Northeast Woodlands and Iroquois Beadwork

Huron Embroidery

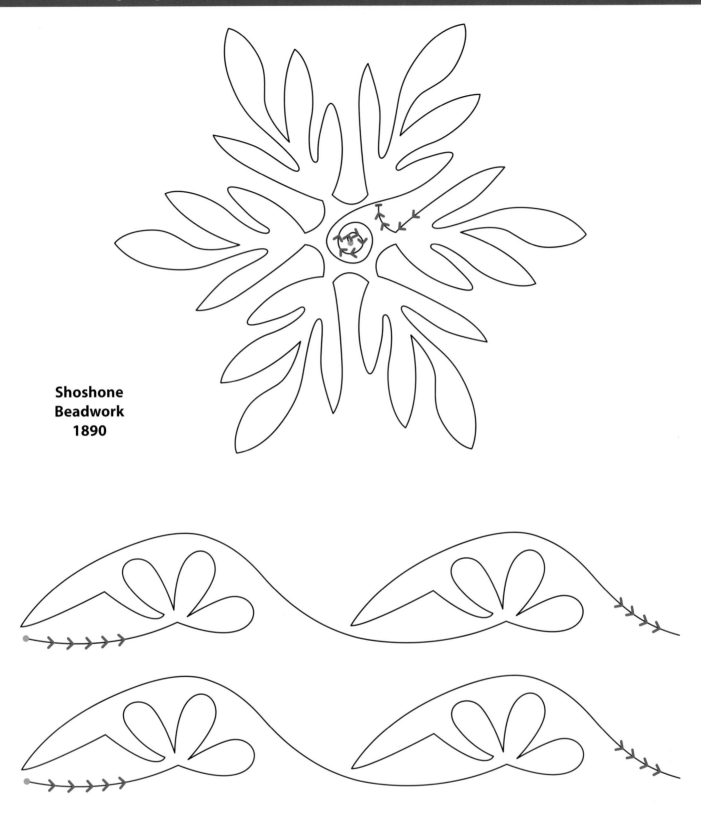

**Shoshone
Beadwork
1890**

**Zuni Pottery
late 19th century**

Acoma Pottery
(dashed lines
indicate
optional fill)

**Prairie or
Woodlands
Beadwork**

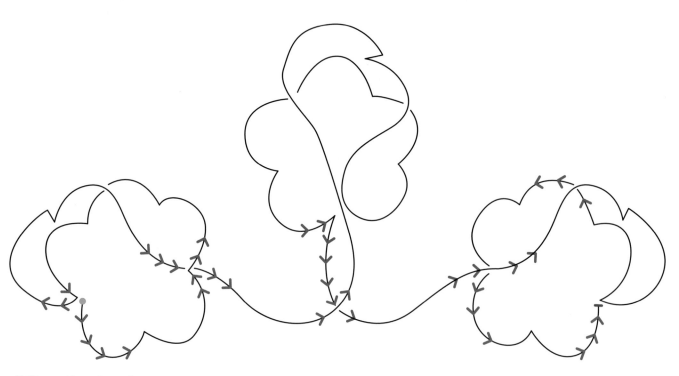

Ojibwa Beadwork
(for a triangular
shape)

**Oto-Missouri
Beadwork
late 19th century**

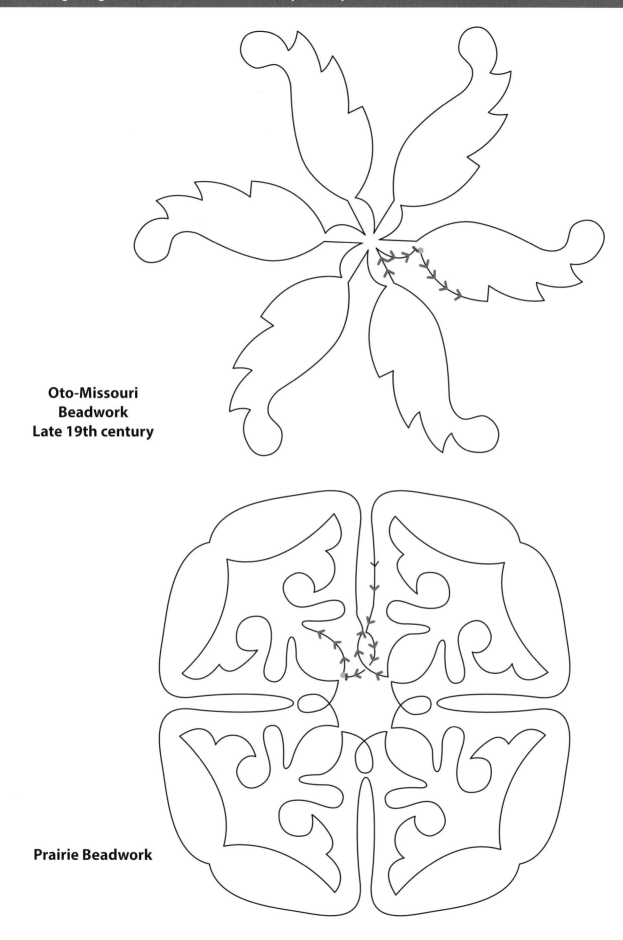

Oto-Missouri Beadwork Late 19th century

Prairie Beadwork

**Historic
Southwest
Pottery**

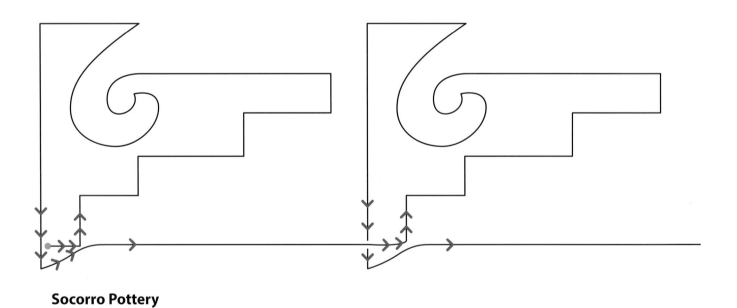

**Socorro Pottery
1200AD**

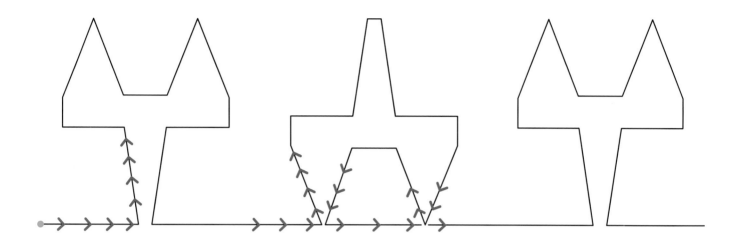

Washoe Basketry

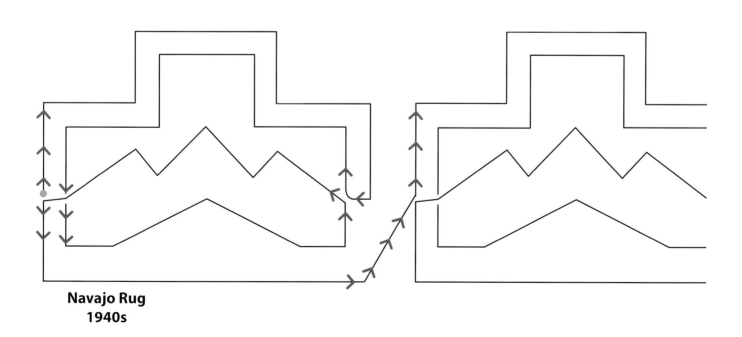

**Navajo Rug
1940s**

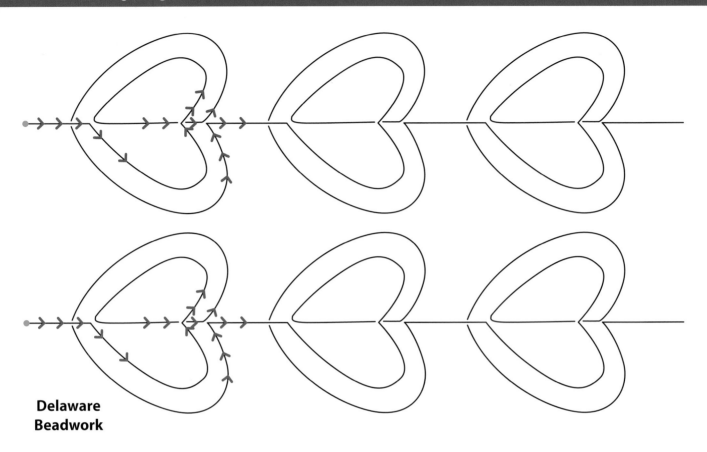

**Delaware
Beadwork**

**Athabaskan
Beadwork
1920–1930**

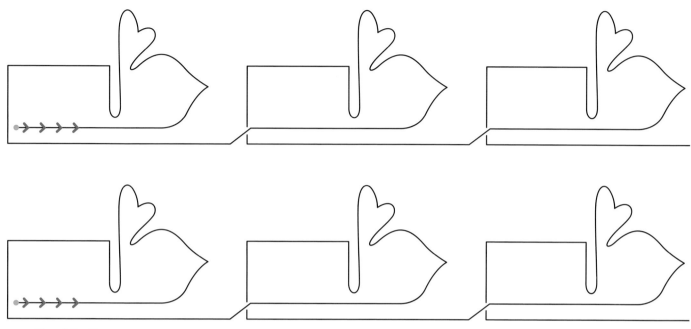

**Zuni Pottery
early 20th century**

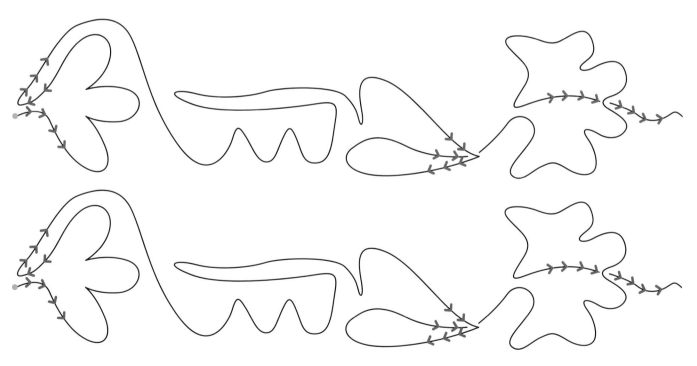

**Tlingit
Beadwork**

Santa Ana Pottery
(dashed lines
represent fill if desired)

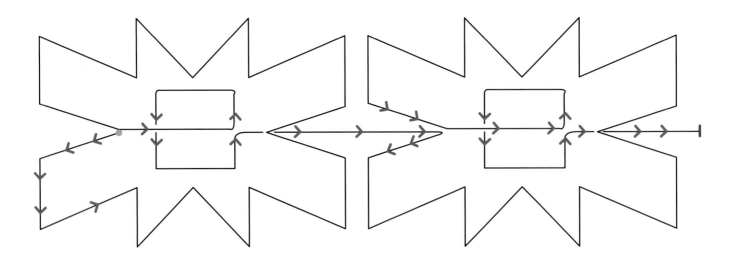

**Plains/Plateau
Parfleche**

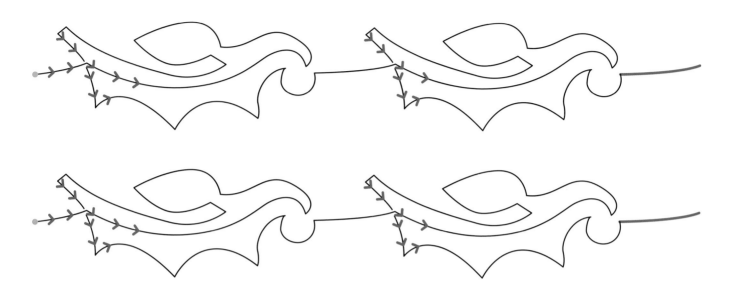

**Woodlands
Beadwork**

**Black Mesa Pottery
1100–1150AD**

**Ojibwa
Beadwork**

**Seminole
Beadwork
c. 1925**

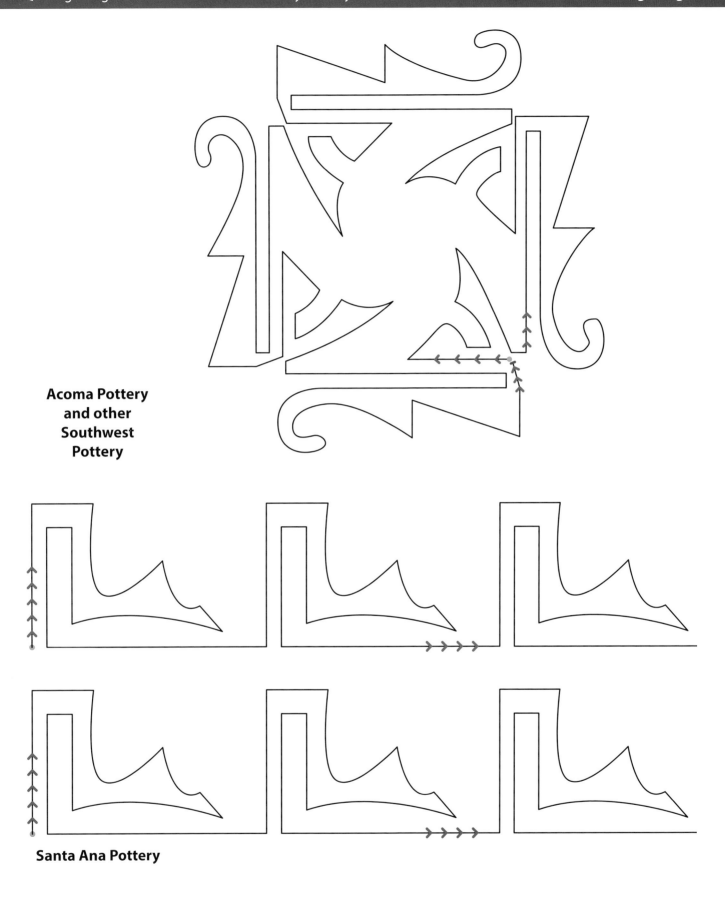

**Acoma Pottery
and other
Southwest
Pottery**

Santa Ana Pottery

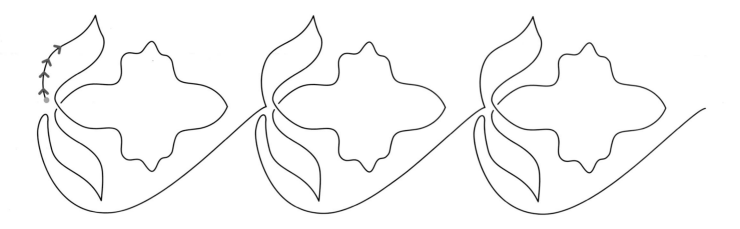

**Potawatomie
Beadwork**

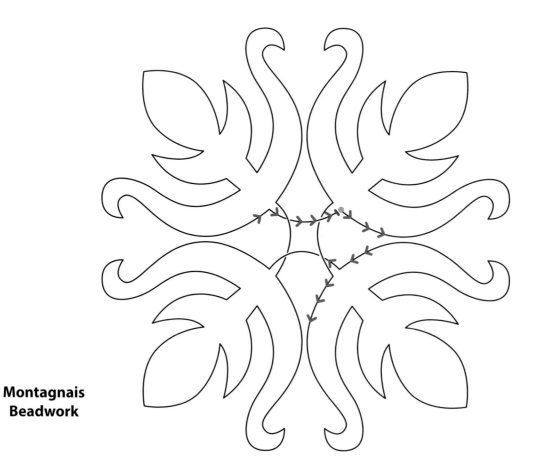

**Montagnais
Beadwork**

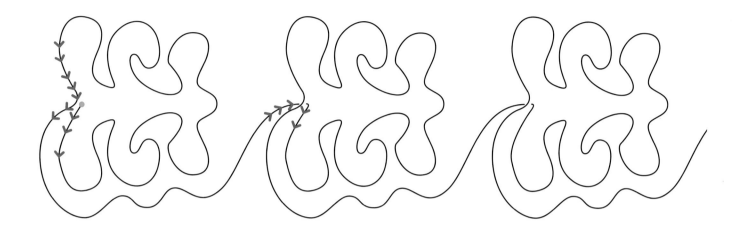

**Woodlands
Quillwork
early 1800s**

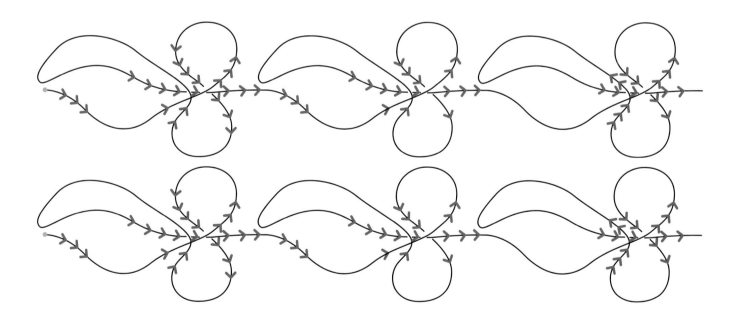

Ojibwa Beadwork

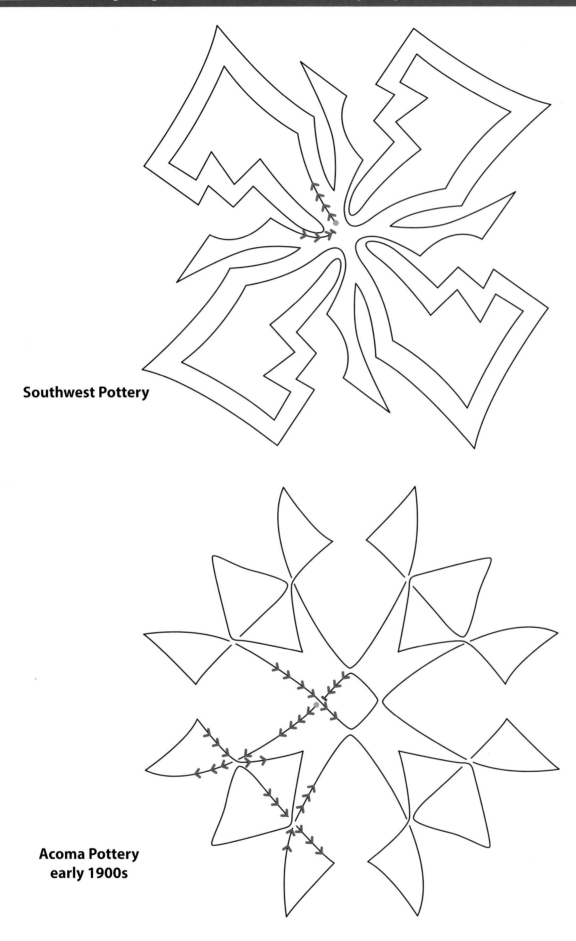

Southwest Pottery

**Acoma Pottery
early 1900s**

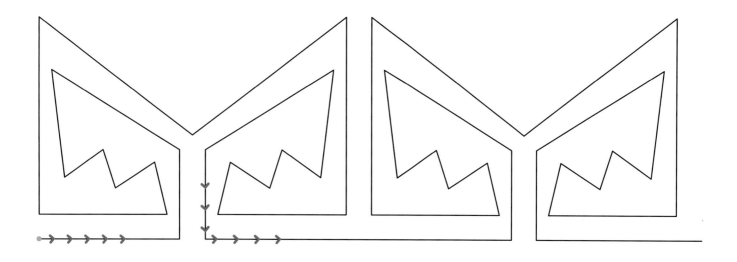

Southwest Pottery

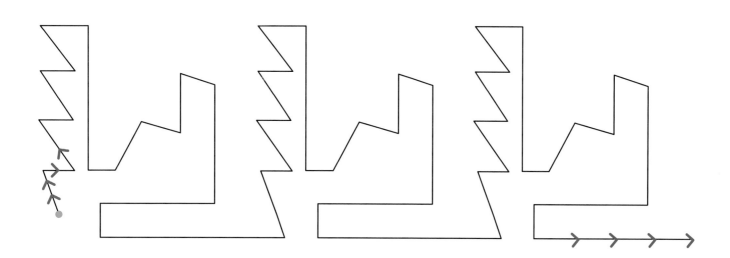

**Prehistoric
Southwest Pottery**

Zia Pottery
(dashed lines for extra fill)

Acoma Pottery

**Delaware Beadwork
early 1800s**

**San Ildefonso
Pottery
early 20th century**

**Woodlands
Beadwork**

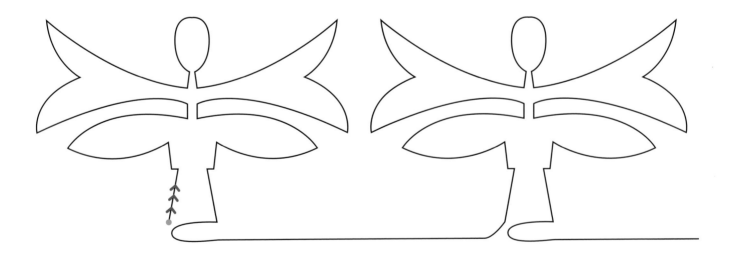

**Zuni Pottery
1920s**

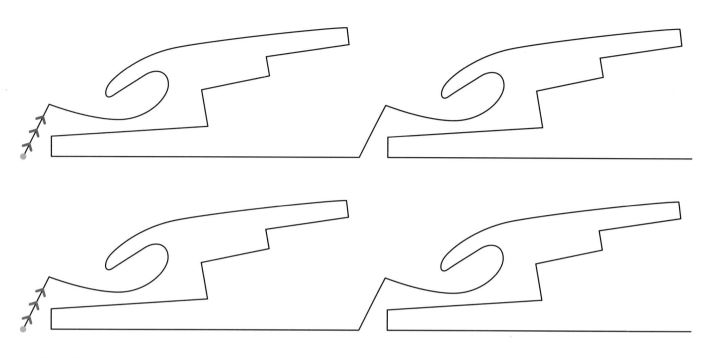

Salado Pottery

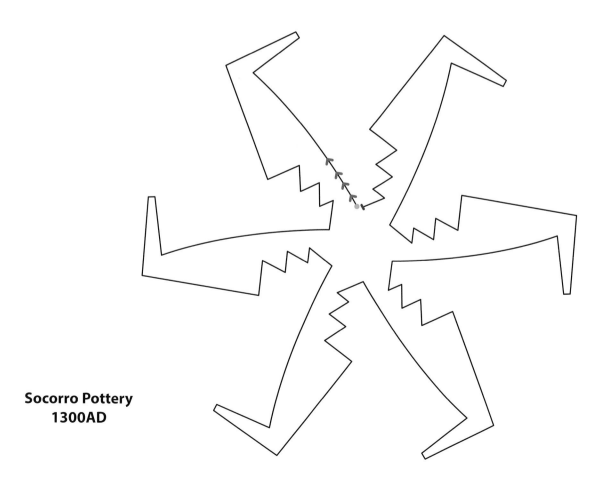

**Socorro Pottery
1300AD**

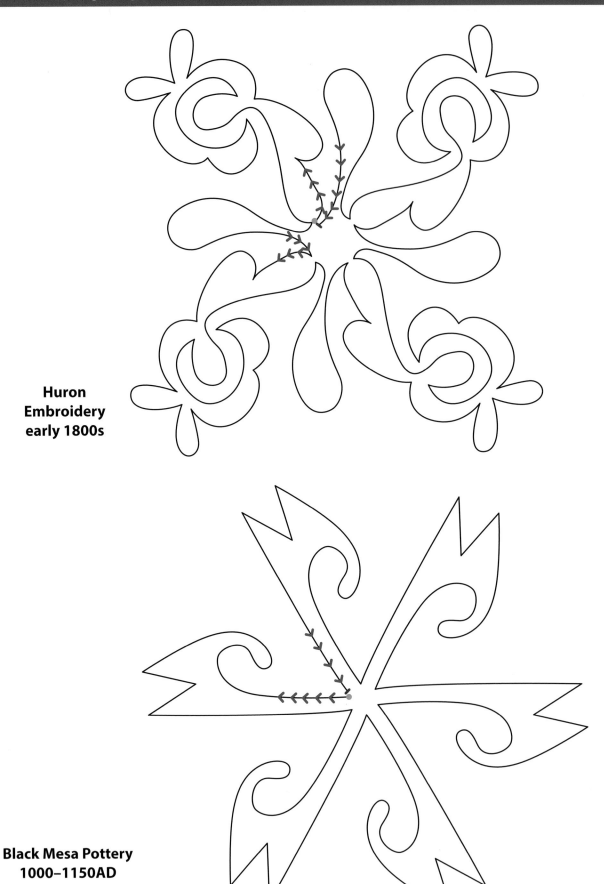

**Huron
Embroidery
early 1800s**

**Black Mesa Pottery
1000–1150AD**

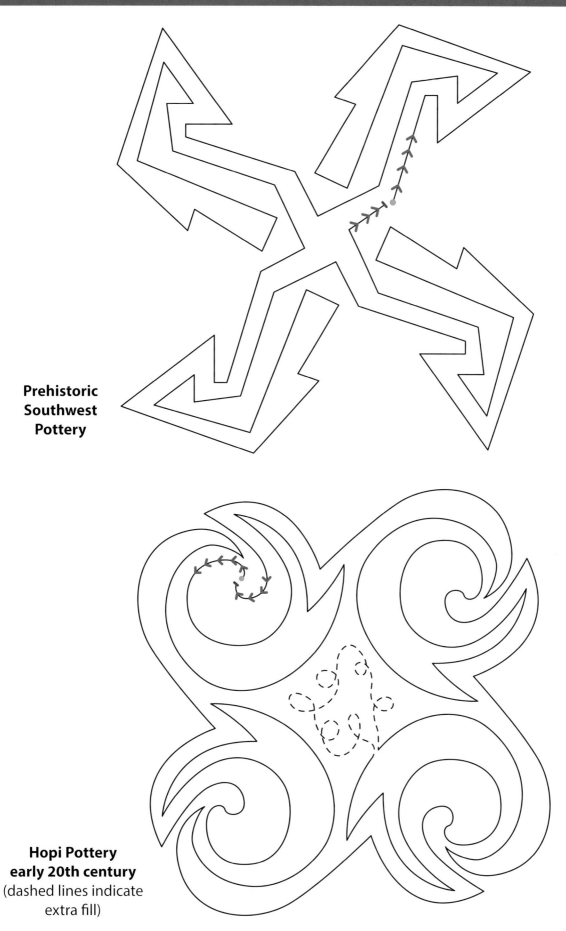

Prehistoric Southwest Pottery

Hopi Pottery early 20th century (dashed lines indicate extra fill)

Plains Woodwork

Iroquois Beadwork

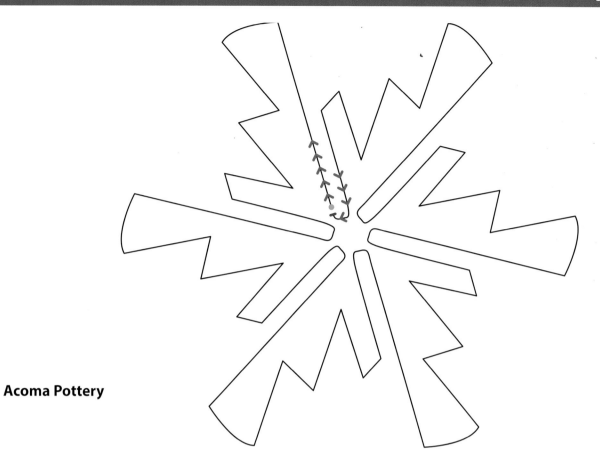

Acoma Pottery

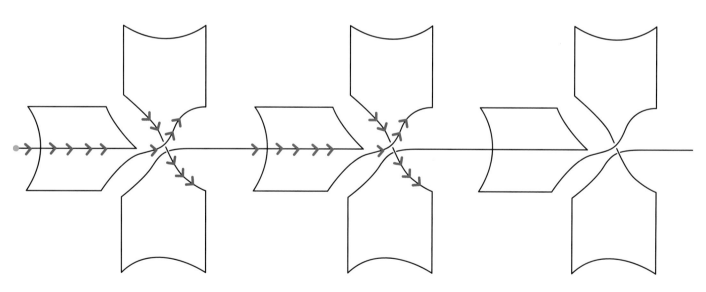

Hupa Basket

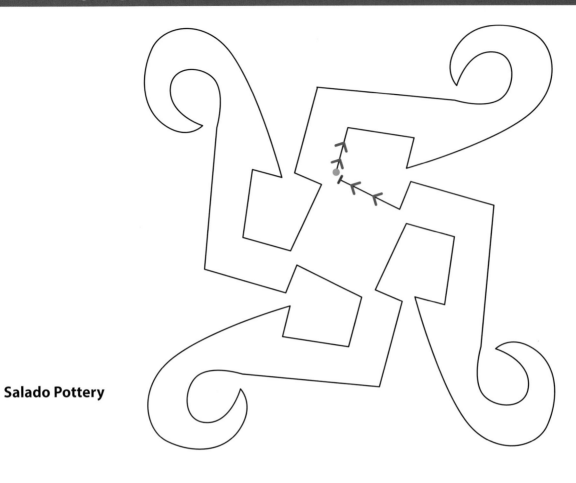

Salado Pottery

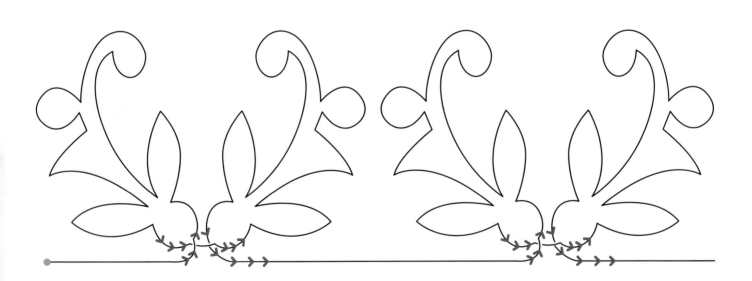

**Santa Ana
Pottery**

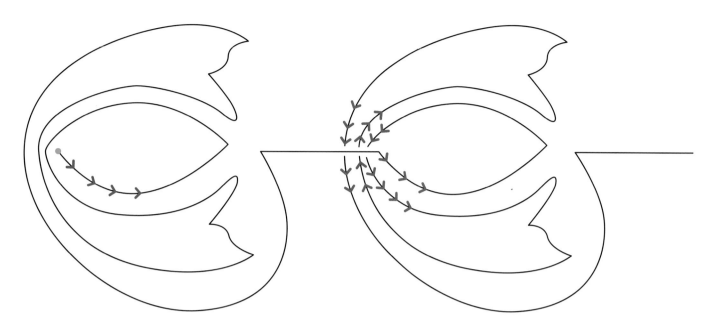

**Montagnais
Birchbark**

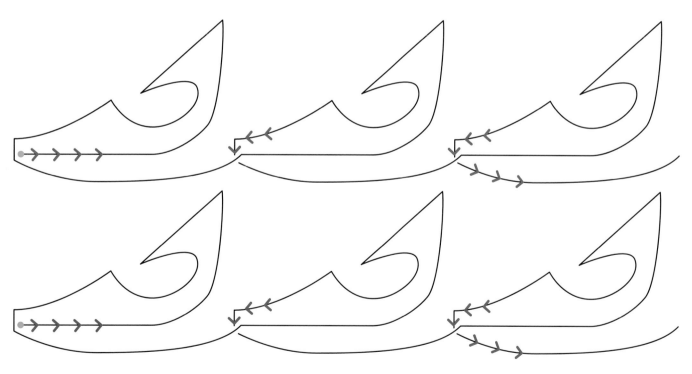

Acoma Pottery

**Acoma Pottery
late 19th century**

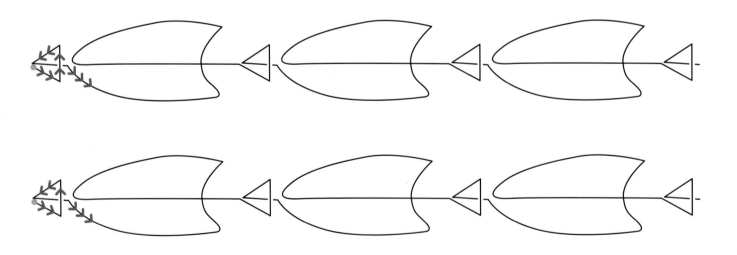

**Plains Indian
Rock Art**

**Acoma or Laguna
Pottery
1860–1870**

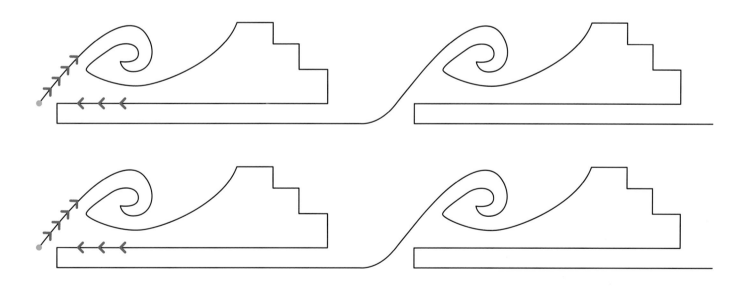

Southwest Pottery

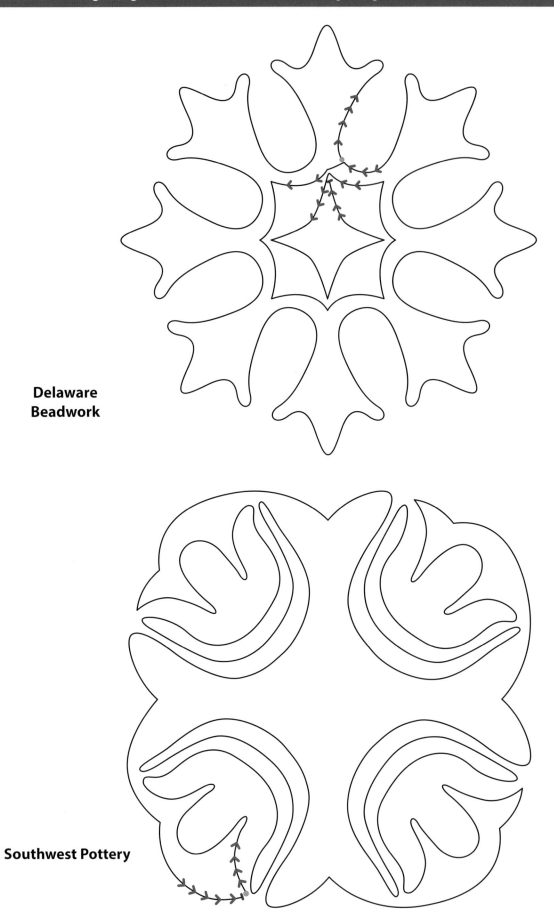

**Delaware
Beadwork**

Southwest Pottery

**Creek Beadwork
early 1800s
and
Kiowa Beadwork**

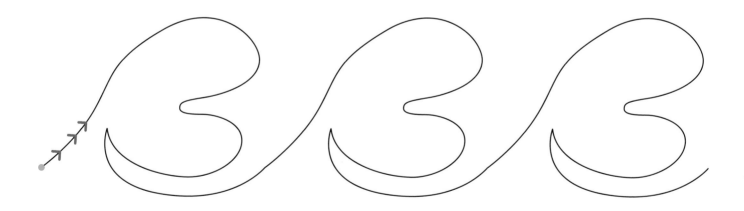

Creek Beadwork

Creek Beadwork
(dashed lines indicate extra fill if desired)

ABOUT THE AUTHOR

Dr. Joyce Mori has been professionally involved in quilting for over 20 years. Her mother introduced her to quilting when she was about 10 years old; her first full-sized quilt was a hand-sewn Grandmother's Flower Garden quilt. She also made some stamped hand embroidery quilts. Eventually, college interrupted her pursuit of quiltmaking.

She earned B.A., M.A., and Ph.D. degrees with a major in anthropology and a specialization in Native American cultures and their technologies. She taught at the college level but made the decision to be a stay-at-home mother.

Once her daughter reached junior high, Joyce returned to her love of quilting and her interest in Native American cultures. She received a National Quilting Association research grant to study the use of Native American designs by quilters, which became the springboard for her career in quilting. AQS has published 6 of her books on Native American designs and quilting designs. She has written 16 books on various quilt-related topics including dyeing and painting of fabric and scrap quilts, as well as technique books on folded squares and more, cutout quilts, and frame quilts, and more than 80 articles on quilting topics.

Joyce has exhibited her work at numerous quilt shows and galleries. She was a West Virginia juried craftsman when she lived in that state, and she has had a line of quilting stencils marketed by Quilting Creations International, Inc.

She continues to visit museums with Native American collections, looking for inspiration, and teaches and lectures at quilt conferences and for quilt guilds around the country.

Joyce and her husband live in central Illinois. She can be contacted at quiltsandminis@yahoo.com.

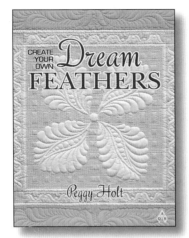

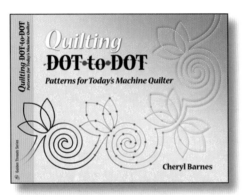